This Book Belongs To

G

There's
NOTHING
SOFT ABOUT
Softball

MY
Heart
IS ON THAT
Field

Softball
SQUAD

LOVE
Softball

SOFTBALL
VIBES

Did
SOMEBODY
SAY
Softball?

Faith
FAMILY
Softball

Softball
MAMA

Love

I'LL ALWAYS
be YOUR
Biggest
FAN

ALWAYS LEAVE
IT ALL ON THE
FIELD

G

LOVE

Softball
IS MY
FAVORITE
Season

TALK
Softball
TO ME

LOOK
Pretty
PLAY
Dirty

Softball Y'all

LOVE

RUN PLAY
SWING
CATCH

Livin' that
Softball
Mom
Life

Somebody's
LOUD
MOUTH
Softball
mama

Made in United States
Orlando, FL
07 April 2025

60279402R00039